How to Stay in Love

How to Stay in Love

Charlie and Martha Shedd

Andrews and McMeel, Inc.
A Universal Press Syndicate Company
Kansas City • New York • Washington

Library of Congress Cataloging in Publication Data

Shedd, Charlie W
  How to stay in love.

  1. Marriage counseling. I. Shedd, Martha,
joint author. II. Title.

HQ10.S49   306.8'7   80-14697
ISBN 0-8362-2900-2

Contents

Notes of High Hope

"How can we *stay* in love?"

For those of us who are married, for the future of all, for our own personal good, is there any more crucial question than: "How do we *keep* the home fires burning?"

Because we believe this is an all-important item on society's agenda, we've been on a long hunt. And what we've found is exciting.

In a day when so many marriages come unglued, we tend to forget the positives, and that's too bad. Why? Because out there in the unreported world, millions of husbands and wives *are* staying in love.

"How are they doing it?"

That's what we've been asking. Through our newspaper columns,* in seminar, workshop, conference, and forum, we've been probing. "Will you tell us your secrets, share your know-how, give us some answers? It could make all the difference."

This book is a report from thousands of happy couples. Blending, melding, enjoying each other (most of the time), they sound their notes of high hope.

Charlie & Martha Shedd
Fripp Island
Frogmore, South Carolina
1980

---

*Editor's note: "How To Stay In Love" is the title of a new Universal Press Syndicate column which appears in papers throughout the United States and Canada. Authored by Dr. & Mrs. Shedd this new feature is the union of two previous columns, "Strictly For Dads" and "Strictly For Moms." In one of those columns they asked their happily married readers to write their secrets for a love which lasts.

"How To Stay In Love," both as book and column, is the result of the tremendous influx of enthusiastic response.

In addition to this source of information Dr. & Mrs. Shedd speak often at special events and conduct a popular forum called "The Fun In Marriage Workshop."

1

Basic Law

"Love Comes Back to the Lover"

"LOVE COMES BACK TO THE LOVER"

Pensive word from Canada:

"When you love someone, it means you want for that person whatever will bring the greatest joy. You want their happiness, pleasure, fulfillment, all the good stuff.

"Is this unselfish of you? Of course not; for the happier they are, the happier you are. When their happiness means as much to you as your own, then theirs is quite as much your own as your own is your own.

"To illustrate: Let's say my wife grills two steaks for dinner, and anyone could tell at a glance which is the superior steak. Knowing that she loves me, I don't have to tell you which steak she puts on my plate. Why? Because more than she enjoys eating a good steak, she enjoys my enjoyment of a good steak. If she ate the better steak, that would be physical pleasure, which is fine, but when she gives it to me, she experiences pleasure of an entirely different order. This is 'spiritual' enjoyment, gratification somehow belonging to a deeper, higher, wider dimension.

11

"But suppose I notice what she has done and the moment her back is turned, I switch plates. Of course, she protests. Yet I override her protestations, insist that she have the better steak, and I am pleased.

"Even a moment's reflection reveals that what masquerades as my unselfishness is obviously the most selfish act I could possibly perform under the circumstances. By insisting that she have the better steak, I have grasped for myself the higher enjoyment of her enjoyment of the better steak." *

A catchy little story of two steaks? Yes, but much more. At the heart of the universe our Creator has inscribed this basic law:

> Giving returns to the giver;
> Blessings come back to the blesser;
> And love sent out circles back in some way to its source.

Those who tune their marriage to this Divine principle have discovered the basic secret to love at its maximum, love as it was meant to be.

Author's note: Throughout this book we have carefully guarded the privacy of our letter writers. In this story of two steaks we made an exception because the author is a writer himself and a famous clinical psychologist. Dr. Keith Floyd teaches "Explorations in Consciousness" at the University of Alberta in Edmonton, Canada. He is especially renowned for a sleep-inducing program described in his book, Sandman's Land. (Tree Frog Press 1976)

One of the most exciting aspects of newspaper writing is that we never know who will be reading our columns. Somehow we always think our fans are extra special people. Dr. Floyd has to be extra special, because the steak story came in response to our request for secrets for staying in love. About the writing of Sandman's Land over a period of thirteen years, Dr. Floyd says, "I could have finished it in ten if I hadn't kept falling asleep."

2
Priorities

Dropping the Good for the Better

DROPPING THE GOOD FOR THE BETTER

Have you ever wanted to issue a declaration of independence? A statement to this effect: All you nibblers at my time, all you sappers of my energy, hear this:

"This day, I do hereby cancel every obligation I have to you."

Tom and Phyllis did something like that.

One night when Tom was on his way to a school board meeting (he's chairman this year), Phyllis was headed out of the house for art class.

As they were saying goodbye, Phyllis made this observation: "Tom, you're such a nice guy. I do wish we had time to know each other."

To which Tom replied, "I was just thinking how much fun it would be to spend the evening with you."

Breathes there a pair with souls so dead, they never to themselves have said: "Why don't we chuck it all and get back to living where it counts."

It can't be done? Or can it?

Tom and Phyllis thought it could. Following their "if only we could" scenario, they sat down together for a hard look at the schedule.

Is this committee really important? And how about that project? Why did we ever agree to head their dumb drive?

Then they began hacking away. He said he would take over the bowing out, make the phone calls, write those letters. She said, "No," she'd handle her part.

So right then she went to the phone, dialed the first number, and their freedom scene was on its way. "I can't tell you how much I hated to give up my Tuesday night bridge club. It really has been a great time with my friends."..."When I resigned from the long-range planning committee at the church, you should have heard the flak. But I just told them I was doing it for some long-range planning of my own."..."I guess what it amounts to is that we had to decide between a lot of good things and the very best."

Some kind of courage, Tom and Phyllis. Thanks for having what it takes to point the way.

Three of the most damning words in any marriage: "Some other time"

Examination on Priorities:

Since "talk, talk, talk" is one of the major secrets to staying in love, the questionnaires in this book are designed to facilitate conversation. This particular questionnaire is to be done together.

A. Together we list our "extras"—obligations outside our home, individual activities, and things we do as a couple:

_____
_____
_____

B. We rearrange the above in order of their importance:

_____
_____
_____

C. Which of our individual efforts could become joint efforts? Of the things we've been doing separately, which ones could we do together?

_____
_____
_____

D. What items on the above list absolutely must be retained?

_____
_____

E. Which ones could be phased out gradually?

_____
_____

F. Which ones might be eliminated right now?

_____
_____

3
Little Things

"Staying in Love
Is a Bunch of Little Things"

EVERY MORNING A LITTLE TOOTHPASTE

"We think staying in love is a bunch of little things. You want a 'for instance'?

"Well, with us, whoever gets up first will roll a little toothpaste on the other's brush and leave it by the sink. We've been doing this almost from the first day of our honeymoon, and when you think about it, you will realize there is a lot more to it than just a little toothpaste. For example, if either of us forgets, it could mean we're slipping. Or maybe some feelings are out of joint and we better do something.

"Do you think a little thing like squeezing some toothpaste could help keep a marriage sharp? We know it can, and in fact we recommended it to our children when they got married, to some of our friends, and to the couples' class we teach.

"Once my husband even gave a little talk about our toothpaste at a sweetheart banquet. What he said was that if more couples would do more little things for each other every day, maybe there wouldn't be so many big problems later. Anyway, squeezing that toothpaste every morning all these years has sure made a big difference with us."

HE GETS THE BABY-SITTER

Dear Dr. and Mrs. Shedd:

You are always saying that the best thing a father can do for his children is to love their mother well. I agree, but I thought I should write, because I don't believe the average husband understands one difference between men and women. This is that women seem to appreciate little things so much.

For example: About three years ago, I stumbled onto one small item which has become a big thing for us. One week when we had to go out for a business engagement, my wife was very busy. So I told her I would call for a baby-sitter. Well, I must say that wasn't as easy as I thought it would be, but I finally did get one.

Right away I knew this was a big deal for my wife. So I decided I should do it again the next time. Then she took off in a cloud that time too, and on an impulse I told her I would *always* get the baby-sitter. You probably know this means I had to start making a list of names and phone numbers, and I keep adding more all the time. I guess no man would realize how baby-sitters have a way of fading out, because girls start dating, or they get busy at school, or their folks move away.

Anyhow I feel better now that I have written you, because maybe there is some husband who needs points with his wife, and he could use my idea.

Here is another thing I might add. The other day I

heard my wife talking to her mother on the phone, bragging about me. Isn't it strange how such a little thing as always getting the baby-sitter would make a woman feel like that?

> Questions for staying in love:
> How can I lower the worry factor for my husband, my wife?
> How can I save him time or free even a few minutes for her?
> How can I ease the drag of routine for my mate?

ACAPULCO AND SAN FRANCISCO

"Yesterday my husband announced that two weeks from today he is taking me on an anniversary trip to Acapulco, but that isn't the big thing. What makes him so unusual is that when David told me we were going, he also told me he had made all the arrangements, like someone to take care of the children; and he has also lined up a neighbor to care for the houseplants, feed the gerbil, and change the water for the goldfish.

"I guess maybe the reason I appreciate this so much is that last month my best friend's husband took her with him on a business trip to San Francisco, but he forgot to mention it until two nights before they were going. It wasn't a surprise trip or sudden or anything like that. He knew all along he was going, and he was planning all along to take her, but he just plain forgot to tell her. You probably know what happened. She pan-

23

icked. She had clothes to get ready and a hair appointment. And who could she get to stay with the children? Things like that. I actually felt sorry for her.

"Well, you can see the difference, can't you?"

FIFTEEN MINUTES' NOTICE

"I'm a hobby craftsman, and recently I made a discovery I thought might help some other husbands.

"For years Harriet would get really upset when she called me for dinner and I wouldn't come right away. If you're a woodworker, you know how it is. You can't always stop right now. If you're glueing joints or something like that, you've got to take a little longer.

"So this went on and every time it happened, she'd be ticked off.

"Well, I got this new idea, at least for me it was new. By just a little thinking ahead, when I started one of my tricky jobs, I'd go in the kitchen, find out when dinner would be ready, and unless it was ready right then, I'd ask if she could give me fifteen minutes or whatever. That way we could time it together.

"You wouldn't think a little thing like this could make so much difference, but it sure does."

For any couple, another good question:
    Would even a little planning ahead be a good
        thing for staying in love?

4
Surprises

**Hot Lunch
and
a Peanut Butter Picnic**

SERENDIPITIES

There is something wonderful about a marriage filled with surprises. "Serendipity" is a beautiful word meaning "finding a pleasant thing, not sought for."

Why would serendipities be such a plus for staying in love? One answer is that a surprise says, "You are so special I have been thinking how I could please you." Is there anyone of right mind who doesn't want to be special? Answer: No one. Since this is true, when we keep our marriage alive with surprises, we are moving toward the basic human feeling, "I want to matter."

And here is another plus to the serendipities: They keep life interesting. Boredom is no threat to the couple big on serendipities.

Why?

"I never know when Larry will bring home something he found somewhere and say it made him think of me. I never know when he will do some little thing he has never done before. Of course, I try to be that way for him, too. And do you know what I think? I think this is one of the reasons why we are so crazy about each other."

SHE FIXED HIM A HOT LUNCH

There comes a time in every marriage when we'd best quit talking and start doing. "Verbal appreciation" is important and it's a barren relationship where there are no accolades. But then the day arrives when action is every bit as important, or more important, than vocalizing.

In her interesting little book, *A Wide Place for My Steps* (Word 1979), Elizabeth Rockwood tells this story:

"At one time in our lives, Bill went through a difficult period in his business. I began to pray and as always happens when I pray, I became aware of Bill with a new sensitivity. I saw signs of fatigue, strain which I hadn't seen before. I also noticed that he had lost weight. When I inquired about this, he said he didn't have time to leave for lunch, so he just ate peanuts and coffee from a vending machine at the office.

"I felt an inner conviction that I should fix a hot lunch each day and take it to the office. I really didn't want to do this. Sure, I had married 'for better or for worse,' but not for lunch.

"Still the conviction persisted.

"Finally, one day I fixed a hot meal and took it downtown to Bill.

"I suppose no hot little meal carried to a lonely shepherd keeping watch in the craggy hills was ever more warmly received.

28

" After a while Bill's work load lightened and he was able once again to go out at noon. Some months later, in a small group at church, the question came up, 'When was God most real to you?' Imagine. My chemical engineer husband amazed me by saying one of his times was when I brought him those hot lunches."

Another good question for every wife, every husband:
Is this one of those days, those weeks, those years when I should add some action to my accolades?

THE PEANUT BUTTER PICNIC

Some men have the knack for doing exactly the right thing at exactly the right time. Bill is one of these, or at least Jackie says he is, and who should know better than Jackie? For fifteen years she's been married to "this perfectly marvelous man" (her words).

"Bill lost his job early in January, just as our Christmas bills were coming in. There didn't seem to be anything we could do about it right away and we were so short of money. Of course, he felt awful and he knew how worried I was, but I want to tell you what he did.

"Even though he was feeling bad, this perfectly marvelous man called me the very next day and invited me out to lunch. It was on the tip of my tongue to say, 'But Bill, we can't afford to go out for lunch.' Then I got this inner nudge that I'd better accept his invitation. So he picked me up and drove me to a little park near my job. We live in Southern California where we can picnic all winter long and he had packed a picnic lunch. It wasn't much of a lunch, because Bill isn't much for things like this. But there we sat on the ground eating peanut butter sandwiches and potato chips and oranges. I tell you it was just like we were kids all over again, and I suppose every couple has certain meals they will never forget. Well, I have a feeling that lunch will be one of our best memories forever.

"Do you know what it means to a woman when her man is so much in charge of even the serious situations?"

HE GAVE UP THE FIRST HALF

What is the nicest thing a man can do for his wife? Possibility, straight from the woman front.

Dear Dr. and Mrs. Shedd:
I am so thrilled I simply must tell you what my husband did.

Last night after the children had gone to bed, Bob sat me down and told me he had decided something. What he had decided was that he would forgo the first half of the Monday night football game. He said not just this week, but every Monday he wouldn't even turn on the TV till time for the second half.

Now that might not sound like much to you, but you see he commutes, so he doesn't get home till 7:30 and sometimes later. Every Monday night for years it's been the same routine. I'd feed the children. Then he and I would sit by the TV and have our dinner. At first he tried to explain football to me, but I never really could appreciate it. Besides I wanted to talk. I wanted to hear about his day, tell him about mine, just visit.

Well, the speech he made was one of the most beautiful things I ever heard. He told me he had been thinking about this, and he decided two things. One was that it couldn't be good for the children to be shoved aside while he watched football. But the best part was the second thing he said and I know I will appreciate it forever. He said, "In the second place, Lucy, after being with the kids all day, you must need some scintillating conversation of the adult kind, and you know how scintillating I can be."

Wasn't that a cute way to say it? And don't you think he really is great?

Staying in love is a bunch of little things, plus *big* ones like giving up the first half of Monday night football.

OVERNIGHT IN LOCAL MOTEL

"You invited us to pass along any good ideas on how to stay in love. Well, I wanted to tell you about the surprise I gave my husband on his December 26 birthday.

"We have been married for twenty-one years, have four children (ages fifteen to twenty), and I am manager of a card and gift shop. In our family, birthdays are a time to say 'I'm glad you were born,' but you can sense what a temptation it must be to let a birthday slide by uncelebrated during the holiday rush.

"So this year I thought up something different. I tried to think of what my husband would choose if he were to have the perfect birthday, and I knew that would be a weekend away with me. He really is crazy about me. Isn't that nice? But I couldn't take a weekend right then what with a half-price sale and inventory coming up, plus company arriving on the twenty-seventh. So why not a night right here in Oskaloosa?

31

"I called our local motel which I'd heard had a water bed. We had never tried a water bed, and was I surprised to know their water bed happened to be in their honeymoon suite, and it was a bargain at $21.

"I purchased a satin robe and pajama set for him and some after shave in a sexy scent. Then on the evening before, I packed his gifts with my most alluring night-gown and hid them in the trunk of the car. I told him I was taking him out for 'a date' and away we went.

"First I took him for dinner and then at 8:30 we pulled into the motel parking lot. I wish you could have seen the look on his face.

"To make a long story short, it was a great success. The room not only had a water bed but also a lighted mirror overhead! For one nice long evening we escaped the turmoil that is Christmas and the kids at home, and business, and friends stopping in, and all the holiday hoopla.

"But both my husband and I would agree that even though it was fun that night, it's been even more fun looking back, talking about it together, sharing it with the kids and our friends.

"Yet best of all, there is no doubt about this: he knows I think he's very special even during the rush times, and I know he feels the same way about me."

TAKING DOWN THE CHRISTMAS TREE, ALONE

What does a woman appreciate most from her man? Mink coat? Luxury car? Trip to Hawaii?
Hear now the truth according to Martha:
"I know one woman who appreciates most the little

things like a husband taking down the Christmas tree. Alone.

"He says it was no big deal, nothing more than a sudden decision he stumbled onto. I was tired. Three days after Christmas I was still resting from eleven house guests. Children, grandchildren, in-laws, miscellaneous door ringers, bringers of gifts, and all the 'merry ho-ho.'

"On this particular morning Charlie got up early, took a look at the tree and decided he'd get it out of the house. Maybe he decided to do it because we had all agreed this year's model was the worst ever. We have a natural tendency in our family to love our Christmas trees, but somehow this one never quite fit the word 'lovable.' Bedraggled, brittle, bare on one side and an endless 'shedder of needles.'

"For a man who had never removed the Christmas tree, the whole process must have been some kind of new experience. Remove tinsel, take off lights, store ornaments, carry out tree, vacuum carpet, clean up room. Then sprawl out for an early morning nap by the fireplace. That's where I found him, and I couldn't help musing. As usual he gave me some very nice presents. He always does each Christmas. I like what he buys me and I like the thoughts, the care, the message behind his giving. But being a woman I know this too in my heart: When the gifts are long forgotten, I will never forget the year I was so tired and he took down the Christmas tree alone!

5
Compliments

"The Warm Fuzzies"

"BLESSED AM I BECAUSE I HAVE YOU"

"Warm fuzzy" is a psychological term appearing these days in the literature on person-to-person relationships. We like it. We use it often and for us it means a compliment, praise, affirmation, the little extras; anything which says, "Blessed am I because I have you."

Whatever the labels, great lovers learn to keep the "warm fuzzies" up front.

When was the last time one of us had to ask, "Do you love me?"

How long has it been since either of us said, "Of course, I love you!"

Is our romancing on the upswing or on the decline?

EVERY DAY A COMPLIMENT:
OLD COMPLIMENTS, NEW COMPLIMENTS

"Marjorie is always telling me I don't praise her enough. At a recent meeting we attended, someone was

37

quoting you two. They said you have a regular system for telling each other what you like. Would you mind repeating whatever it was you said?"

Since almost every mail brings at least one query like this, here it is again.

This is a compact between us and we call it "every day a compliment."

It is evening now and one of those days when we've been concentrating almost wholly on ourselves, our own doings, our own needs. This is the dinner hour, or bedtime, and somewhere in our conversation you would hear the fun little phrase, "I haven't had my warm fuzzy." So it's "I like you because" or some other version of "I am now about to tell you why I think I'll keep you."

Sounds like a game? Sure, but could your marriage use a game? And if you'd make it even a game, would you find what we found? This becomes much, much more than a game. It becomes a kindness of a special kind; and never, absolutely never routine. Was ever a person born who got too much of, "You really are special and now I will tell you why, with meaning!"

"ISN'T SELF-SATISFACTION ENOUGH?"

"Why all this stuff about praise, patting people on the back, telling them they did a good job? My parents brought me up on the idea that if you did a good thing, you'd know it and that's all you need. So isn't self-satisfaction enough?"

One woman's answer:

"Do you know how barren it can be to live with a man who never tells you that you look nice, never says one single word of appreciation. I mean never even the smallest compliment on the way you keep house, how you manage, how you love, not the first good word.

"I guess the reason I'm writing is that last night I asked my husband why he just sits there eating my best offerings (I am a very good cook) and he never says so much as a common, ordinary thank you. So when I asked him 'why?' he said, 'Can't you tell from the way I go after it, I like it?' Well, I wanted to throw the whole lemon meringue pie straight in his face. Of course, I didn't. Instead I went back to the bedroom and had another good cry."

What's the matter? The matter is that self-satisfaction won't do it. Good thing, yes. But never enough!

DOMESTIC ENGINEER

She's a small woman. Cute, freckles, and a big smile as if somebody had turned on lights inside.

We'd been discussing marriage at its best, communication, and how to keep the fun up front. Then said the big man with a grin, "There's no such thing as 'just a housewife.' The lady really is 'a domestic engineer.' That's what I call Ginny and I tell the whole world, 'Meet the most valuable member of our outfit.'"

The "Martha movement" is a national organization with thousands of members in fifty states. It takes its name from the Mary, Martha Bible story and its aim is to give homemakers the status they deserve.

One of their leaders says, "A lot of people, even some of us, feel that what we do is crummy. But we've got to start raising our own self-image. We are homemakers, that's what we are, and homemaking is creative business. Sometimes it's plain hard work making family life successful. And sometimes it's hard work too, helping your husband be successful. So let's come alive, girls. We deserve more than we're getting."

No doubt about it. You do deserve more. So here's today's question for male musing:

Does my wife ever think of herself as "just a house-wife"?

And what could I do to give her the feeling "You're the most valuable member of our outfit, a true domestic engineer"?

SHE'S MARRIED TO A FAMOUS GOLFER

"It does take some doing being a plain Jane, playing second fiddle, living in the shadow of a famous name. You have to get used to your husband bringing home all those trophies, getting all the praise. He's the big hero and you feel like nobody. And you might as well know all those adoring women fluttering around him, that can make you nervous too.

"So how do you manage it? Well, I'm one of the lucky ones and one reason is my husband's attitude. I mean the way he treats me, the things he says. From the very first when he started to win, he would tell everyone how important I am to him. He would say, 'I don't know what I would do without her to keep my books and keep things straight and keep me relaxed.' We would also talk over his game and he would even ask me to study his stroke and tell him little things I'd notice.

"I don't think the average man realizes how much a woman wants to believe what her husband says. If he tells her how good she is where she knows she might be, after a while she comes to accept the fact that she's as good as he says she is. As a matter of fact, I actually do believe him now when he tells me, 'Except for golf, you can do everything better than I can.'

"If you've seen our pictures together, you've probably noticed I'm smiling most of the time. That's what people say anyway, 'She's always smiling.' Well, I wasn't like that at first, but that's another thing I owe to my husband. He keeps telling me I have the most beautiful smile in the world so I should keep smiling. And do you know I have come to believe he's right about that too. My smile *is* the most beautiful smile in the world *for him*."

Questionnaire on the Warm Fuzzies

Since "talk, talk, talk" is one of the major secrets to staying in love, the questionnaires in this book are designed to facilitate conversation. Unless otherwise indicated, we suggest that you each answer the questions on your own separate papers. Then if your marriage is ready for it, study each other's answers, compare notes, and set a time for discussion.

1. The last time I paid my mate a compliment was_____
2. The type compliment my mate likes best is_____
3. Five things I especially like about my mate are:

   _____
   _____
   _____
   _____
   _____

4. This list would come as no surprise to my mate, because I verbalize these things and I verbalize them often.
       Yes_____
       No_____

5. Some things I like about my mate but have never expressed are: _____

6. Words are not the only means of expressing appreciation. I let my mate know I am grateful by specific things such as: _____

7. After thinking through these questions, my performance grade for expression of appreciation is:
       Excellent_____
       Average_____
       Poor_____

6
Talk

Staying in Love
Is Talk, Talk, Talk

TALK, TALK, TALK

Is it okay to admit (even a little) that life when you were single had its good side too?

We had known Sophie as a friend and she had come for advice. The question? "Is it all right sometimes to wish you weren't married?"

Her husband was on military assignment. The Orient. Two weeks from today he'd be returning and now she was surfacing some troublesome thoughts. "A part of me likes his coming back and a part of me doesn't. The truth is I rather enjoy this independence, the freedom to come and go as I wish. Like for instance, I can cook what I want without thinking of him, and I can also cook nothing at all if that's how I feel.

"Yet I'll also be glad to see him. Real glad. I like the security he gives me, the smell of his pipe, the way he laughs. But I feel so divided. One part of me wants to go on living the way I am now, and the other wants to go on the way we were. Is it so wrong for me to feel like this?"

So he came back. We lost touch for a time. Then some months later they were reassigned and we saw them again. They seemed to be the same happy couple we'd known originally, so we asked them how they'd accomplished their return to normal.

The report:

"After that short honeymoon feeling, it was awful. We were really not very nice, saying ugly things, rebelling. Then one day we decided to face it. We'd both enjoyed some things alone, but we really did care about each other too. So we discussed our feelings long and hard and often; we began to make some adjustments; and now because of what we've been through, we are even closer than we were before."

Same song, next verse. In almost every marriage problem the answer is *talk, talk, talk.*

EVERY WEEK A DATE

Every week a date for Charlie and Martha.

Forty years multiplied by fifty-two weeks makes two-thousand-eighty visits outside our home!

Away from the children, away from the doorbell, away from the phone. Two-thousand-eighty times shutting out the world, concentrating on each other, verifying our love, talking, talking, talking.

You can't afford dinner out every week?

Maybe a picnic? Hamburgers? Your favorite ride? Dessert, coffee, a walk through the park?

Thought for starters:

The money we spend for a weekly date is *not* an expenditure. This is one of our most important investments.

SMALL NOTEBOOK SOLVES MARITAL PROBLEM

Are we talking enough at home about what happens during our day? And if we aren't, how can we develop some intelligent way to share what we're doing at work?

One answer:

"My wife and I saw your request for ideas on how to stay in love and we decided I should tell your readers how we corrected a problem we had.

"Our marriage got off to a bad start, partially because I didn't talk enough, and especially I wouldn't tell my wife all she wanted to know about my work. I am in a high-pressure job and I like to forget it when I get home. But there are other reasons why I didn't talk. For instance, I have always been sort of a private person about my worries. Then I had also been listening to the wrong advice. By that I mean I have an uncle I looked up to. Before we were married, he told me, 'When five o'clock comes, turn off your job. Never take it home with you.'

"So here was my wife asking questions, wanting to know what kind of a day I had, and I was refusing. I not only didn't want to think about it, I told myself she was trespassing on private territory.

"Well, I finally got the message. I decided I better make some changes and here's how I did it.

"I got a little notebook and whenever something happened at work I thought she might enjoy, I would jot it down and take my notes home with me.

"You can't imagine what a change this made in our marriage. Anyway, we agreed I should write you in case there are other men who need a practical suggestion for changing. I would also like to say that my little notebook, in addition to solving this problem with my wife, has even helped me like my job better."

HOW GOOD ARE YOU AT SELF-ANALYSIS?

How good are you at self-analysis?

Shirley lives in Pennsylvania, but the way she looks at her own problem could be a winner anywhere.

Dear Dr. and Mrs. Shedd:

One day last month I was with some of my friends in a planning session for our Junior League. All of a sudden I heard myself talking to these very intelligent women exactly as I would to the twins and they are in fourth grade. If you know Junior Leaguers, you know most of them are very intelligent people. So of course, when I realized what I had been doing, I was embarrassed. After the meeting, I told my best friend how I felt, and she said, "Shirley, what you don't know is you do it all the time."

This bothered me even more, so I decided to do something drastic. What I did was to have a real heart-to-heart talk with my husband. He said, "You even talk to me like that sometimes." Then I told him I thought the reason I was sounding like a juvenile was that I needed more time for some adult conversation, and would he help me.

He promised to give it a try, so here's what we do. Every night after dinner, we plan it so he and I can sit alone and talk for thirty minutes without the twins. Maybe it can only be ten or fifteen, but sometimes we get into a subject when we go on longer. I can't tell you the difference this has made.

Questionnaire on Talk, Talk, Talk

Since "talk, talk, talk" is one of the major secrets to staying in love, the questionnaires in this book are designed to facilitate conversation. Unless otherwise indicated, we suggest that you each answer the questions on your own separate papers. Then if your marriage is ready for it, study each other's answers, compare notes, and set a time for discussion.

1. We talk as much now as we did when we were first married.

   Yes_____

   No_____

2. The actual amount of time we talk with each other daily would average_____
   Even though there are days when our talk-time is brief, our weekly total would average _____

3. The last time we had a heart-to-heart talk was _____

4. I don't talk more because:
   a. In my home we learned not to tell everything_____
   b. My mate questions me too much_____
   c. When I talk, I get too much advice_____
      Or a putdown_____
   d. Too many things I tell may be used against me later_____

5. Sometimes I talk too much.

   Yes_____

   No_____

6. The subjects we talk best about are:

   _____

   _____

7. Subjects I would like to talk about:

   _____

   _____

7
Listening

"You Be Her Psychiatrist"

AFFIRMATIONS FOR A LOVING LISTENER*

1. I will try to concentrate on what you are saying. I will train myself to put my work aside, the paper aside, anything aside, and turn off what I'm thinking to focus on your words.

2. I will try to feel what you are feeling. This may be hard, but I will sincerely make the effort to get behind your words and experience what is in your heart.

3. I will give you a chance to say it all. I will hold my tongue and not comment too soon.

4. I will try to prime your pump. I will ask questions. Sometimes I will say back to you what you have said until we both understand fully what you mean.

5. If I feel even the smallest anger from you toward me, I will try my best to control my fire.

*From How to Know You're Really in Love by Dr. Charlie Shedd, Andrews and McMeel, Inc., 1979. $6.95

6. I will not cop out by giving no answer when an answer is important. I will remember that silence is sometimes effective, but sometimes it's cowardly.

7. When you are hurting because you're down on yourself, I will assure you again that no matter what you think of you, I am still *up* on you.

THE COST OF LISTENING

"I was paying this jerk fifty dollars an hour for listening to my wife."

Dear Dr. Shedd:

Driving to work this morning I thought I ought to write you about something that happened to me last year. You are always writing on treating the kids' mother right. I sure agree with that, but I learned the hard way how important it is.

What I mean by the hard way is that last year my wife was seeing a psychiatrist every week. And even though our insurance carried some of it, it was really tearing up our budget.

The psychiatrist and I belong to the same club. So one time over drinks I was telling him what I thought about that fifty dollars an hour, which wasn't getting any easier, believe me.

So he says, "Don't blame me, stupid. You're paying me fifty dollars an hour to listen. That's all the lady needs. No big problems, just lonesome. You want to save all that money? So take a little time every day to listen and I do mean every day. Really listen. Let her talk. Take her out for dinner, every week take her out. Let her talk some more. You could be doing what I'm doing. You be her psychiatrist. Give it a try. Besides saving all that money you're griping about, you might find out what a nice person she is. Maybe you'd even have some fun!"

Of course, he used a lot of long words I didn't understand. But I'm giving you my version, and would you believe it worked!

Then listen to this: For a while now my wife has only been going once a month, and last week the doctor told her he didn't think she needed to come anymore. Wow!

"WHAT I HEAR YOU SAYING IS..."

Dear Dr. Shedd:

My wife and I have discovered six words which have made a fantastic difference in our marriage and we would like to pass them along in case others might be able to use them the way we have.

Our six words are "What I hear you saying is..." and here is how it works. Whenever one of us is getting our temper up or saying something negative, instead of snapping back, we will use these six words, "What I hear you saying is...." Then we repeat what we thought they said.

Why does it work so well? For one thing, it keeps us from jumping to conclusions and it also helps us not to take everything personally. Then it enables the other person to clarify their thought when they hear it back.

I don't think we fuss any more than the average couple, but I can tell you for sure, things are a whole lot more peaceful around here than they were before.

"STAYING IN LOVE IS ALSO 'SHUT UP'"

"In case you think every wife has trouble getting her husband to communicate, I thought I should tell you my story. The trouble with Ronald is he won't shut up. Honestly I think he starts talking when his feet hit the floor in the morning and he never stops until he goes to sleep at night.

"I tell you that can be hard to live with too. Right now it's hard for the children, especially at dinner. When they have something to say about school or their friends, I feel sorry for them. Have you ever heard anything like this before? And what can I do about it?"

So what can she do? Chances are she can't do much until Ronald is willing to find out what causes his logorrhea (psychological term for running off at the mouth).

For husbands, for wives, for all of us, there might be real merit in musing on these words of the wisdom writer:

"There is a time for keeping quiet." Ecclesiastes 3:7, *The Bible in Basic English.*

8
Disagreeing

Learning to "Fight Right"

It was a short note, one paragraph:

> "Dear Charlie,
>   I hate you.
>   Love,
>   Martha"

A real shocker, especially for me. I went into marriage with the mistaken idea that lovers should always be in love, always have positive feelings for each other. But experienced lovers know that love at its best is also being honest; sharing those negatives which could later disturb the relationship.

EYEBALLS, ELBOWS, AND KNEES

Who has an effective method for surfacing hostility? This Kentucky husband says he knows one.

"For 'eyeballs, elbows, and knees' husband and wife sit opposite each other with knees touching. Then they put their elbows on their knees and hold hands. Now they look each other in the eye and say, 'I am about to tell you what is bothering me.'

"You would not believe what all you can say to each other in this position. Also it is almost impossible to be dishonest now, and because you are touching, there is a feeling of closeness which you need at times like this.

"There is one more thing. You are less likely to turn each other off. As you sit there together like that, you don't mind asking questions and you are more likely to get it all out.

"Anyway, my wife and I have been doing it often for several months and we are beginning to get to the bottom of some real problems. We strongly recommend it, and we believe any couple trying it will find it effective."

"CHALLENGE"

The Allens have an effective method for sharing their differences, surfacing disagreements.

Dear Dr. and Mrs. Shedd,

We've been married ten years and, at first, like most couples, it was just great. Then gradually things started to go in a different direction. We think what happened is that we got a little bit scared when we began to disagree. Then we made our first mistake. Instead of talking these things out, we kept them inside. Of course, that only made things worse.

Well, we didn't really like that so here comes what I think somebody else might want to hear. We decided to work out a system by which we could disagree with each other. We call it "Challenge" and now I will tell you how it goes.

When one of us is about to say something negative back to the other, instead of saying "You're wrong," we will say "Challenge." That means we don't agree and we're serving notice that this needs some discussion. It is so much better for us than some of the things we used to say.

Isn't it surprising what one little word can do?

CHALLENGE!

THE COMMITTEE

Pat and Jennifer are both hot-headed. That's what they say. They're also the kind who tend to fight things through to the finish. But this tendency was strictly no good when they were first married, so here they tell us what they did about it.

"We agreed to a deal where either one or both of us could say, 'Let us refer this to the committee.' Whenever we say this, it means that we don't feel like fighting right now. We're tired, we've had a hard day, this is no time to settle the argument. Let's deal with it later.

"Then when we are feeling up to it, one of us can say, 'How about that committee meeting?'

"For us it's been great. If you are like us, you better not hide your uglies, because they will probably burn you up and you feel just awful. But referring it to the committee lets you know it won't need to bug you forever. Also there is another advantage. It gives you time to get it all sorted out and line up your arguments. Or maybe before you get to the committee meeting you will even see how silly you were in the first place."

HOW TO "FIGHT RIGHT"

"Does anyone have any kind of a deal for how to 'fight right'? Margie and I get along great most of the time, but when we don't, oh brother!"

The speaker was a big, warm-looking redhead, but he might have been any size and any like of looker. Why? Because almost every husband has his moments of ire and every wife her hostility.

So now to some helpful thoughts on how to "fight right." These come from a perceptive wife and we like them so much, we think they're worth sharing.

"Let me tell you something interesting one of our boys said recently. One night when we were all into a serious conversation, he asked, 'How come you folks don't fight? Seems like so many of my friends' moms and dads yell at each other and some of them even throw things. How come?'

"When we thought about that, we realized there actually were some reasons we don't fight the way others do. And when we began sharing our reasons with the boys, we decided maybe our reasons might mean something to someone else if we told you about them.

"To begin with, we had to admit that we do have our differences, we do disagree, sometimes very much. But two things happened early in our marriage which set certain limitations we think were important then, and still are.

"Once when Rex was very angry, he shook me, and I told him, 'Don't you *ever* do that again. Don't you *ever* touch me that way any more,' and he never has.

"Then it wasn't long after that, that I walked out when we were having an argument. That's when he said, 'Don't *you* ever do *that* again,' and I never have.

"So those are two of our more dramatic answers, but there are two more. And here they are:

"We have an understanding we'll never call each other names in anger.

"And we will try never to say anything we would regret later. This keeps us from that ugly recall which is going to hurt over and over. We think that's important too, because when you are through with these things you should really be through.

"Maybe these four behind-the-scenes agreements in our marriage will help some other couple over their rough spots."

THE BOOMERANG OF TEMPER TANTRUMS

Dad tells mother off.
Mother gets back at dad
   by taking swipe at Johnny.
Johnny takes out his feeling
   by cuffing dog.
Dog senses something wrong,
Chases cat up tree.
   Guess who goes for ladder
     to scale tree
     and rescue cat.
"Hi dad! Still mad?"

Questionnaire on Sharing the Things We Don't Like

Since "talk, talk, talk" is one of the major secrets to staying in love, the questionnaires in this book are designed to facilitate conversation. Unless otherwise indicated, we suggest that you each answer the questions on your own separate papers. Then if your marriage is ready for it, study each other's answers, compare notes, and set a time for discussion.

1. When something comes up I don't want to discuss:
   I change the subject_____
   Clam up_____
   Blow up or react negatively some other way_____

2. When I was a child, I was taught to think for myself and encouraged to disagree intelligently.
   Yes_____
   No_____

3. I have done some careful thinking about my mate's background as it relates to disagreement:
   Yes_____
   No_____

4. I think our early histories here might be worth discussing together.
   Yes_____
   No_____

5. Are we too uncomfortable with disagreement between us?
   Yes_____
   No_____

6. Most of our disagreements are caused by:
   _____
   _____
   _____

7. What ground rules could we adopt to surface our hostility?

   _____

   _____

   _____

9
Loving the Unlovable

"I'm Still Up on the Basic You"

LOVING THE UNLOVABLE

For staying in love nothing can ever be quite so effective as learning to return positive for negative.

It was a major day in our marriage when Martha sat me down one evening and said, "Charlie, something is wrong with you and you're not being nice to me. You have been snapping at me, growling at me, saying things I don't think you really mean. If you'd like to tell me where you're hurting I'm willing to listen, but I want you to know even when you aren't at your best, I still love you. No matter how much of a downer you're in, I'll always be up on the basic you."

Long, deep, forever, a man will be praising the Lord for a woman like that!

Then came the day when *she* hit the emotional skids. When this happens, my normal reaction is panic, pushiness, verbal clobbering. But this time, at a strategic moment, I remembered what she had said to me. So I moved in on her darkness now with all the affirmation I could muster. "Remember, you can never get so down on yourself, on the world, on me but that I'm still up on the basic you."

Easy? Never! This kind of love requires the putting aside of personal feelings, discipline, control, waiting. Then more of the same, more selfless loving till the sun comes through.

High country this, and it's a long climb. But any couple who has made it up here knows that the view is worth whatever it took.

Loving the unlovable—one of the truly great secrets for staying in love!

"EVEN WHEN WE'RE OWLISH"

Stuart and Polly quit smoking. Three months now they've been off the weed and it hasn't been easy. Some couples say, "No problem," but not these two. Stuart still reaches in his pocket often, and Polly says, "I think what I miss most is our after-meal smoke or lighting up together anywhere."

So what's the message? The message is that Stuart and Polly did something worth passing along. When they made their decision to kick the habit, they had what they called a "head session." They said, "Being the kind of people we are, we knew this wouldn't be easy. So we faced it. We knew we were sure to be owlish, and we'd be taking it out on each other. That's why we made an agreement not to take it personally when one of us got bitchy. And we decided too that we would even try to be nicer to each other when we weren't uptight. That would be sort of like creating a reservoir of good feelings which we could draw on later.

"So what we would like to say is that when you know you are going to have a hard time, it may help you to preview the whole thing like we did."

Tough times coming up?
If we take an honest preview now
and make a recommitment to our love
would we come out stronger
at the end of this tunnel?

"NEVER GO DUET IN YOUR MOODS"

"When we first married, Gretchen and I had a problem with our moods. If either of us got moody, it upset us too much. Then one day we discussed it, and we decided part of the trouble was opposite backgrounds. In her family she was supposed to be high all the time, so she felt guilty when she wasn't. I was from a family of stoics. You know what I mean? Never let anyone know your feelings. So we talked it over, and decided right there we should each be natural.

"We also agreed to try something we saw in one of your columns. What you said there was, 'Don't go duet in your moods.' That meant a lot to us and we are working hard on it. When one of us is down, the other makes a real effort to stay up. That is one of the best things we ever agreed to."

ALL THE GOOD THINGS

Dear Dr. Shedd:
    We read your column regularly and I want to tell you

about my husband, because maybe you'd like to tell other readers something he did last week.

I had really messed up. I won't go into details, but it was something I said at a party when I should have been keeping my mouth shut. I was so embarrassed, in fact I was mortified.

When I was feeling the worst, Jim took my hand, made me look him straight in the eye, and then he said, "Sue, I know you blew it. You know you blew it. So what? I've blown a few and we'll both do it again. But I want you to know I haven't forgotten all the good things you've done. I'm thinking of those, and maybe you should too."

Do you know how much a wife loves a husband like that?

And vice versa?

10
Apologies

"I'm Sorry. Forgive Me"

"I'M SORRY. FORGIVE ME"

"Even Jesus Christ said nobody was good but God. Well, my husband happens to be a preacher but I guess he doesn't really believe that verse, because I have never once heard him say he was sorry. He refuses to even entertain a flickering thought that he might have done something wrong or made a mistake or been in error any way.

"Can you imagine how hard it is living with someone like this?"

From the beginning of time, refusing to accept blame has been a human characteristic. When the Lord asked Adam, "Why did you eat the forbidden fruit?" Adam came back with, "It was the woman's fault." So what did Eve say? "The serpent talked me into it."

"Projection" is the psychological name. It means passing the buck, pointing the finger. "My husband," "my wife," "those folks," anyone but little old me.

But projection is never the answer. "I did it." "It was my fault." "I'm sorry." "Forgive me." These in varied version, and often, are absolute essentials for staying in love.

Questionnaire on "It Was My Fault. I'm Sorry"

Since "talk, talk, talk" is one of the major secrets to staying in love, the questionnaires in this book are designed to facilitate conversation. Unless otherwise indicated, we suggest that you each answer the questions on your own separate papers. Then if your marriage is ready for it, study each other's answers, compare notes, and set a time for discussion.

1. In our marriage, do we tend to blame each other? "It's his fault." "She started it." Alibis, excuses, pointing the finger, by whatever label, too much of the time we're guilty of these.

     Yes_____

     No_____

I am guilty of all this.

     Yes_____

     No_____

My mate is more guilty than I am.

     Yes_____

     No_____

2. In the home where I grew up my parents set us a good example. They apologized to each other and to us and we were taught to admit our failures.

     Yes_____

     No_____

3. The last time I apologized was _____

4. The one area where I have the most trouble facing up to my errors is _____

     Others _____

5. When we have a quarrel, which one of us is more likely to move toward reconciliation? _____

6. When my mate apologizes, I can accept it gracefully and put it away.

     Yes_____

     No_____

11
Flexibility

"Staying in Love
Is Zigging and Zagging"

"What do you mean zigging and zagging?"

We were in a couples' seminar and the theme here was how to stay in love. So when he said what he did, the group egged him on.

"Well, I mean over the long haul you better learn to sidestep some things, to give in when it means more to the other person than it does to you. And even when it means a lot to you, you better give in sometimes. That's what I mean by zigging and zagging."

Adaptability.
Flexibility.
Stretch.
All important words for staying in love "over the long haul."

POSTERS IN THE DEN

Are we fussing unduly over things which really don't matter "all that much"?

Dan and Amy are very independent people, but also very much in love. She is a design specialist with an advertising firm and her specialty is posters. She creates them big, splashy, colorful and sometimes "loud, loud."

During the first months of their marriage, Dan says he almost blew his cork when she brought home her handiwork and hung it in their den. She would sit back, admire her latest creation, and of course, ask him for his reaction.

"But I soon caught on," says he. "She didn't want my observations much. What she really wanted was for me to admire, tell her how great she was. It was rough going, I kid you not, and especially because I didn't want them in the den no matter how well I liked them. Some of them were 'loud, loud' and I always thought a den should be casual, comfortable, quiet.

"Can you imagine the first night I walked in? Bam! Well, I was about to open my face with 'Oh no,' when I felt this nudge from somewhere. 'Maybe she needs this, and does it really matter all that much?'

"So I decided to put up with it awhile, and now it's ten years later. But here is the bottom line.

"Last week when we were having a group in, Amy decided to take her posters down, every one of them. Don't ask me why. She just took them down, all of them. So what happened? I could hardly believe it. The kids really got on her, and me right behind them. Then we all talked her into letting us put them back up.

How's that for a switch?

"And you know something else I've decided? Sometimes if you can keep your mouth shut, some things you didn't like at first will do a complete turnaround. Isn't that amazing?"

MOLLY LEARNS TO BOWL

If you were married to a "bowling nut," how would you cope?

Molly is the mother of Greg, thirteen, and Gretchen, nine. But by her own definition her husband is a "bowling nut." Nine months a year he bowls every Tuesday, every Thursday, no exception.

He also bowls Saturday mornings now, and here's how that happened, straight from Molly.

"I'm a beautician. Five days a week I'm running my own business, so I have to plan real carefully for family time. And you can believe I resented Don taking two nights a week to bowl. Well, I did what I shouldn't have done. I nagged and I pouted, and I got mad, but it didn't do one bit of good. Actually, it just made me feel awful.

"It was my mother who showed me what was happening. She said, 'If you can't beat 'em, join 'em.' Then she suggested a plan and I decided it might be just the thing.

"What I did was to cut out two or three appointments every week, and during that time I took bowling lessons. To keep it a secret I went to an alley Don never goes to, and I did that for six months.

"Believe me, I'll never be a prize bowler, but when I got respectable, I invited Don to go bowling with me Saturday mornings. You can imagine how surprised he was, but I knew he would go for it, because it gives him more time to sharpen his game.

"Of course, he gives me a handicap and once recently I almost beat him. One day I'm going to. Anyway you can't know the fun we have, and every Saturday when we finish bowling, we go to lunch together.

"Because I know there are a lot of women with problems like mine, I wanted to tell you my story."

"If you can't beat 'em, join 'em!"
Giving up the tap, tap, tap of verbal hammers, doing a switch, making friends with the inevitable is plain good sense for certain situations.

Run them by again: Flexibility, elasticity, stretch, zigging and zagging. All these may be just the thing sometimes for staying in love!

"THE FAULT FACTOR"

Moose is a successful driller of oil wells. He's been at it thirty years and he's "crazy enough to like it." That's what he says.

"I guess you've got to be a little bit touched to be a driller in the first place and crazy enough to like it. But it sure wasn't that way the first few years. I'd go berserk when one of my rigs broke down. You know what I mean? I'd be worrying about all this money I'm losing. Then an old boy told me, 'Moose, you'd save a lot of wear and tear on your insides if you'd allow for a fault factor. I mean everything you do, any time, any year, any month, decide you're going to have some trouble. Ten percent, twenty, sometimes thirty percent of the time something will go wrong.'

"So I decided to figure it like he said and there is just no way I can tell you the difference it made.

"Then I began to apply this fault factor thing in the family. My kids, they couldn't be perfect with the dad they've got. Allow for a fault factor! And my wife. She's a great gal, really, but she's not perfect. So why get so uptight, Moose? That's what I keep telling myself now and, like I say, this fault factor thing sure made a difference."

Questionnaire for the Fault Factor

Since "talk, talk, talk" is one of the major secrets to staying in love, the questionnaires in this book are designed to facilitate conversation. Unless otherwise indicated, we suggest that you each answer the questions on your own separate papers. Then if your marriage is ready for it, study each other's answers, compare notes, and set a time for discussion.

1. Those things my mate does which irritate me most are:
   _____
   _____

2. The way I handle these irritating things is to:
   Blow up_____
   Shut up_____
   Speak up_____
   Other _____

3. It seems the things I do which most often irritate my mate are:
   _____
   _____

4. The way my mate handles these irritants is to:
   Blow up_____
   Shut up_____
   Speak up_____
   Other _____

5. We could improve our relationship if we made more allowance for the fault factor in each other.
   Yes_____
   No_____

6. We could make some changes here if we did these things:
   _____
   _____

12

Freedom

"I Am a Person, Not a Thing"

"BUT WE'RE SO DIFFERENT"

"But we're so different."

Say it again, Sam, and you too, Susan. Say it again every Tom, Jane, Mary, Bob, and anyone married to anyone.

Usually when we hear it, the meaning is heavy with negatives. "See how impossible it is for us to blend!" And often the hidden meaning comes through as one more excuse for calling it quits.

Yet "we're so different" can be loaded with positives too, if we learn this one thing:

Differences keep life interesting.

Mary Ann is a high-school senior. On breaking up with her long-time steady, she said, "Everyone was surprised when we split and especially my folks didn't like it, because they're crazy about Mike. Well, I am too, but do you know what he and I decided? We decided we're too much alike and even though we'll always be good friends, we agreed it would probably be better if we married someone different. You know, more of a challenge?"

One great statement from Mary Ann and Mike. Love does get something extra from shaping, adjusting, stretching.

Exercise for all marrieds:

First we read I Corinthians 13 (often called "the most beautiful words ever written on love").

Next we ponder a long time on the only repetition in this entire chapter from I Corinthians: "We know in part."

Finally, we thank God for our differences. Because we aren't exactly alike our life together can be more interesting.

WOMEN DON'T THINK LIKE MEN— AND VICE VERSA

"No matter what the unisexers say, women don't think like men. They don't react like men, and a guy better know it."

Word from a recently married husband who adds, "Before I caught onto this, there was big trouble."

And a young wife writes:
"It took me a long time to understand that Stan is thinking about business so

much of the time when I'm thinking about our relationship, the children, things here at home. So many times in order to get his attention I feel like I'm calling across a chasm. Then I remember how he is and things go better."

LET THE LADY CRY

"Ernie and I have only been married six months and we are having a hard time about my crying. I was brought up in a family where I was encouraged to cry. Sometimes my parents would say, 'Go ahead. Have a good cry. It will make you feel better.' So I would cry, and I would feel better.

"But Ernie actually goes all to pieces whenever I cry. Even when it doesn't have anything to do with him, he can't stand it. He follows me around and asks what's the matter. He may even say, 'Don't be such a baby.'

"I have tried to tell him I'm the kind who even cries when I'm happy or when I hear something sentimental and why doesn't he quit worrying."

THE CRAZY SLEEPER

Meet Maggie.

By her own confession, she's a "crazy sleeper." She always goes to bed when Tom does. But then she gets up in the night to read, knit, hook rugs, listen to records. During the day she takes little naps. Thirty minutes, twenty minutes, ten.

Report on the current situation, straight from Maggie:

"The first few years we were married, Tom was constantly nagging me about my sleeping habits. 'It's just not normal, Maggie. You'll kill yourself.'

"So finally, I sat him down and gave it to him straight. 'Listen, Tom, I've been this way all my life, and I'm not about to change now. You've got to admit I'm a good housekeeper and a good wife. You couldn't handle any more loving than you're getting from me, so I've heard the last I want to hear from you about my crazy sleeping. From now on Maggie is going to be Maggie.'"

THEY JOG IN DIFFERENT DIRECTIONS

Barney and Jane are joggers. They've been jogging for almost two years and they're in great shape.

So what else is new? Many couples jog together. Only the news here is that Barney and Jane don't jog together. They do their running in a park near their home; they run at the same hour, but they run in opposite directions.

Now why would they run that way?

Here's the answer straight from Barney:

"When we started jogging, we did it together like other couples. At first we rather liked it that way, stayed right with each other for support. But gradually, we began noticing that things weren't going so well, and the reason was simple. Jane likes to run fast. I like to run slow. The experts say it doesn't really matter, because you get the same results either way. So we talked about it, and we decided we would go in opposite directions and both set our own pace.

"Jane goes like crazy doing her laps and I poke along taking all the time I need to think through my day. Jogging isn't a time for visiting anyway. So we howdy when we meet and that's a nice little touch.

"And here's another big thing we decided: It's not very bright for us to do everything together just because other people are doing these same things together. We're different people even though we're married, and our marriage is different from every other marriage. We like it that way."

Good question for any couple:

> Are we doing some things with each other just because other people are doing these things with each other?

One more time:

> Would our relationship go better when we *are* together if we quit straining for togetherness?

THE SUBMISSIVE WIFE

Often these days women ask, "Should I let my husband have his way in everything?" And the question usually originates out of some right-wing religious scene.

Among these groups there is heavy emphasis on a single verse from the Book of Ephesians (Ephesians 5:22). It says here, "Wives, submit yourself to your husbands." Some of the modern translations shade into harder interpretations, "Let him have his way in everything."

So what's wrong with this emphasis?

What's wrong is that it takes one verse out of context and manipulates womankind to man's advantage.

Too often overlooked is the verse preceding "Give him his way in everything." The words in this verse (Ephesians 5:21) are "Submit yourselves *to each other.*"

So if we are to submit to each other, the logical question is "How?"

One answer for us is facing the fact that every person on earth is sometimes ineffective. Why then should we operate under the delusion that we need to be at one-hundred percent efficiency one-hundred percent of the time?

Martha: "Charlie, you are not thinking straight. Turn off your head. Temporarily, I mean, let me do the thinking for us. Today, I'll make whatever decisions need to be made. Then one day when I'm down and you're up, you take over."

It's a mutual art and a great one, this learning who should submit, when to submit, and how to.

So they are wrong who say a woman should always give in. Sometimes she shouldn't. Each of us is here as surely as any one of us is here and each has rights as surely as anyone has rights.

Always for the great lovers, one of the great secrets is submission in duo.

> Archie Bunker's attitude is well
> known to fans of "All in the Family."

His classic explanation: "In the
Bible it says 'God made woman from
man's rib,' and everyone knows the rib
is a cheaper cut."
Important question
for any husband:
Is there something of Archie,
even a little, in my thinking?

THE WOODS AND THE ART GALLERY

"I work in a factory where there is a con-
stant noise all day from machines pounding
and clattering. In the background there is also
the hum of powerful electrical equipment.
And whenever there is any conversing, it has
to be in a loud shout.

"Perhaps all this is why I have learned to
appreciate the woods. Every weekend when
I can, I spend time in the woods, and if there
is a weekend when I don't get to the woods,
I can tell you it's no good.

"But my wife doesn't share these feelings.
She is a different type. For instance, she likes
to go to art galleries and I think they're nothing but dullsville. At first we had some real
problems trying to work this out, but then we
faced it. She'd never like the woods the way
I do and for me art galleries would always be
awful. So we compromised and it was really
very simple. I go to the woods. She goes to
art galleries.

"What's wrong with that?"

HOW MUCH DOES IT MATTER WHAT THE NEIGHBORS THINK?

"I'm married to a woman whose big thing is yard work. She loves flowers, bushes, plants, trees, dirt on her hands, and she especially likes to mow the lawn.

"So what's the problem?

"The problem is a neighbor who talks too much. For instance, last week at a barbecue the old dowager asked me why I didn't buy Helen a riding mower. Well, Helen likes the exercise she gets walking behind the mower.

"So I told this pushy broad, 'Listen, I bought Helen a new electric mower because that's what she wanted. So why don't you go soak your head?'

"Sure, I felt kind of guilty sounding off like that and I guess I should have explained that on the days Helen mows, I take over some of the housework. I actually do like to dust (a little) and straighten up, and cooking is one of my favorite things. Maybe I should have told the old gal all that too. But then again, if a man and his wife can work it out the way they like it, why shouldn't a nosy neighbor go soak her head?"

MUTUAL MINISTRY

Audrey is a young Tennessee wife, struggling. She writes:

"Can a man ever get over thinking of his wife as a servant? Is it even possible for him to change?

"Wayne and I have been married four years and we get along okay some ways, but one part of our relationship is simply awful.

"I think the reason is that Wayne came into our marriage thinking everything would be just dandy now, because I was going to cater to his every need. Well, I have needs too."

Then she goes on for several pages concluding with the question: "Can a man ever get over thinking of his wife as a servant?"

Answer: Yes, he can get over it, and I know, because that's how I came into our marriage. My mother waited on me hand and foot. "Anything you want now, Charlie?"

Wrong?

Sure, it was wrong, but that's how she did it. So here I was now with another woman to cook for me, wash my clothes, pick up, even sleep with. Hurrah.

But then one day Martha leveled with me. (Lesson in Women's Lib.) "Listen, Charlie boy, let's get this straight. I am not simply an extension of your ego, or an appendage to your career, or your servant. The best kind of marriage is mutual ministry. Get it?"

I got it. Gradually, slowly, sometimes painfully, the message came through loud and clear; "The best kind of marriage is mutual ministry."

Question to improve by:
What habits carried over from my past
might prevent a better blending?

AFFIRMATIONS FOR HEALTHY FREEDOM

Throughout our marriage there have been times when we have tended to coercion. At one stage, when we were headed again into this "You do what I want and that's cooperation," we took what we call a "deep think" and out of that came our affirmations for healthy freedom.

1. We will remember that each life here was created by God with certain inalienable rights.
2. Since this is true, as we deal with each other, we will allow plenty of room for each to develop basic individuality.
3. We were trained in general ethics, morals, right and wrong; and we will live by that code. Yet at the same time we will understand that each must develop a personal code too.
4. Because we trust each other, we will allow the other to do some things without reporting; to go certain places without explaining; to live some areas strictly on the basis of "to each his own."
5. Respecting each other's privacy, we will not overquestion or unduly pry.
6. Since our kind of freedom requires serious consideration of each other's anxiety, we will aim to live by the Golden Rule.
7. We accept the fact that our marriage did not just happen. We believe that we are (both individually and together) a part of the Divine Plan. Therefore, both individually and together, we will measure our lives against that larger background of responsibility to the Lord.

Questionnaire on Freedom

Since "talk, talk, talk" is one of the major secrets to staying in love, the questionnaires in this book are designed to facilitate conversation. Unless otherwise indicated, we suggest that you each answer the questions on your own separate papers. Then if your marriage is ready for it, study each other's answers, compare notes, and set a time for discussion.

1. How does the freedom thermostat at our house register?
   Too much freedom?_____
   Too little?_____
   Just enough for staying in love?_____
2. In what areas do I tend to coerce, to push, press, and try to reshape my mate? _____
   _____
3. In what areas do I feel pressured to change?_____
   _____
4. "Wedlock" is an ancient word with positive and negative meanings. What does it mean to me? _____
   _____
5. "Let there be spaces in your togetherness" is a meaningful statement by Kahlil Gibran. By this statement on the scale of 1 to 10, I rate our marriage _____
6. We could have a better relationship if we would quit straining for so much togetherness.
   Yes_____
   No_____
7. In order to relieve the pressure I would need to:
   _____
   _____
8. I think my mate could relieve some of the pressure by ___
   _____

13
Work

A Mutual Philosophy of Labor

JOE AND ANGELA—
ON WORKING TOGETHER

Can a couple work together and still stay in love?

From Joe and Angela, one loud "yes." And they have thirteen years to prove it.

Joe and Angela run a resort motel. When they married, Joe quit his job (automobile mechanic) and Angela resigned as hostess in a fashionable restaurant.

If you could see them doing their thing together at their resort on the lake, you would say, "Smooth. Super synchronization."

But it hasn't always been like this.

Angela says, "Our friends thought we'd lost our minds, our family told us we'd never make it, and during those first few months we wondered if they were right.

"We didn't know thing one about the resort business and it definitely was some kind of awful. We were really

101

messing up, getting in each other's way, but the worst part was our relationship and how it was going downhill so fast. Well, we had both been married before, so we took a hard look at what was happening and decided we had to make this one go.

"What we did was to reorganize the whole thing. First we took inventory of what we each liked best, what we could do well, and where our weaknesses were. Then we divided up the work. I took over the books, the reservations, housekeeping duties, running our little grocery, ordering supplies. Joe was in charge of the marina, the docks, bait, boats, motors, gasoline, repairs to the buildings, the walks, the roads, the yard. Then we agreed we would keep out of each other's way. And we really did it.

"We also have another secret. Even though we don't eat breakfast together, or lunch, we insist on a couple of hours alone every night for dinner. Unless there is a serious emergency, the help simply will not interrupt us, because they know this is our time for each other."

Straight from the work-together front:
We will face the facts
Preplan
Make some definite agreements
Then we'll keep out of each other's way.
But we won't forget either to allow some time for the right kind of togetherness.

REVERSING ROLES TO STAY IN LOVE

He hasn't worked in five months and it may be five months more before he goes back. His name is Paul.

He's a factory worker and we hope not many of us ever need to go through what he's going through. But whether we do or don't, what he says merits a second look and perhaps some serious discussion.

"My wife and I have been through something we wouldn't wish on anyone. But we also think the way we're handling it might be worth telling in case there is someone who could profit from our story.

"Five months ago we discovered I had a heart problem. Because it will require some delicate surgery, the doctor says I shouldn't do anything but rest and it will take several months waiting, building me up, before I'm ready.

"Without going into details I will just tell you that I am a factory worker with a specialized trade and it is not one for a weak heart. So, of course, I had to take a leave of absence. Fortunately, my company does allow for sick leave and has some benefits, but with a reduced income, my wife had to get a job.

"Can you imagine how a man feels when he has been the sole support of his family, but now his wife goes off every morning to earn the bread?"

"So there I sit, doing nothing, feeling sorry for myself, watching all that dumb TV, wondering about the future. Well, I've got to be honest. It was hell and I became a real jerk in my attitudes and I knew it and did my wife ever know it!

"Finally, the two of us sat down for a long talk and she said, 'If you can come off your macho even a little, I will teach you how to cook and dust and make beds. I will also show you how to do the laundry, and get the children ready for school.'

"So what else could I do? I took her up on it and here

103

I am five days a week doing what every housewife does. I guess I should tell you I was a hockey player and if you'd ever seen me play, you'd get a better picture of how this whole thing looked at first, I mean to me and to both our families and our friends.

"I tell you it wasn't easy for a lot of reasons. I never had any idea how much it takes to keep house right. In fact, it was such a surprise to me I decided I better check with my doctor, but he said it might be just what I needed. Well, that's how it's been; a good thing for me and for my wife and for our marriage. I also think our children have a new respect for me and we all get along much better together now than we ever did before.

"So this is why I wanted to write you, because we have proven to each other, and to everyone, that people can keep a good thing going through rough times if they will face it together and determine to make whatever changes have to be made."

SHE WANTS TO GO TO WORK NOW

"My wife and I have been having this big argument. She's thinking about going to work for a tax firm. She did that before we were married, and now that our children are in school, she wants to get back into it. The problem is all the men in our family earned the living. We grew up believing that a woman's place is in the home. I have a good job, she has everything she wants, or almost everything. So why won't she settle for that?"

Have you ever considered this possibility? She won't settle for that because she shouldn't settle for that!

For long-range staying in love, something like this is always a part of the credo:

We care so much for our togetherness that we cherish our individuality.

And because we do, we will make the adjustments necessary for us *both* to feel like contributors—useful and fulfilled.

PREPARED TO EARN HER OWN WAY

Long titles are very much in if they get the message across and here is one of the longest we've come on recently:

How to Go to Work When Your Husband Doesn't Want You to and Your Children Are Too Small and You Can't Do Anything Anyway.

We read it to our coffee-time friends the other day. This one was.

When we finished laughing, Tony took over: "Maybe it's not so funny, guys. You know what I think? I think a man owes this much to his wife. He ought to be sure she's ready if anything happens to him, or even to their marriage.

"My sister was divorced last year. Two kids. No support from her husband and what can she do? So what did she do for a living before she married? Get this: she was a model, but you ought to see her now. No way! There she is, absolutely out of it. Working at a dull job. Pure drudgery, poor pay, no money to go to school and when would she do it anyway?"

Some speech, Tony. But that wasn't all.

"You know what we decided, Rachel and I? We decided we'd both feel better if she'd get herself prepared. So right now we're trying to save enough to send her to nursing school. She's always wished she could be a nurse, always been good with people. Sure, it'll take two years, maybe three. But I'm telling you, in this day and age if a man really cares, he'll be sure some way, somehow, his woman is prepared."

14
Money

A Policy You Can Live With

"IF WE ONLY HAD MORE"

"When it comes to money, it's really not how much you have, but whether you have a policy you can live with.

"We kept thinking if we only had more, that would solve everything. Then we got more, and you know what? We only had more trouble, because we were making the same mistakes, just bigger now."

THOSE LITTLE BROWN ENVELOPES

Dear Dr. and Mrs. Shedd:
The title of this story might be "Love Those Little Brown Envelopes." You are asking how to stay in love and we thought you should know about the brown envelopes because they made a big difference when we were first married. And now they are serving the same purpose for our son and his wife.

David and Shari have been married ten months and they live near us. Having married children close is not always a good idea for either the parents or the children, but in this case we think it was good because we could see they were headed for big trouble. And most of their problems were money problems.

David was raised to know the value of his dollar and how to spend. We trained him to budget, to keep accounts, and not to overspend. But Shari doesn't know the first thing about budgeting or keeping bills paid and she spends money like it is going out of style. I have a good job so we bailed them out a couple of times, but my wife and I knew this was no good. We could tell the children didn't really like it either. In fact, we felt it was hurting our relationship with them.

So we decided it was time to do something and here is what we did. We sat down together, the four of us. We took their total income (they both work) and together we roughed out their approximate costs in various areas. Then we gave them some brown envelopes and had them label each one. "Groceries." "Clothes." "Utilities." "Rent." "Entertainment." "Church." "Miscellaneous." Everything like that.

As I said, this was not new to us because we used the envelope system when we first married. For some reason, however, we had never thought to tell any of our children how we did it or how it might help them.

Anyhow what we wanted you to know is that we think it's going to work. It's been four months now and we can tell already it is doing some good. Shari seems to make a game of spending the contents of those envelopes, juggling, borrowing from one envelope to use in another. Also it is very apparent that David isn't nearly as nervous as he was and we think we know why.

All of this is the reason we decided we should have our say on staying in love and it is also why we say "Love those little brown envelopes."

HE LEFT HER IN GOOD SHAPE, OR DID HE?

Virgil and Stacey were among our favorite friends, and *were,* regretfully, is the word. Virgil is gone now from a sudden heart attack. He left her in "good shape." That's what everyone said. But was she really in good shape?

Virgil was a sharp businessman, made money, and there must be plenty of residue. But why would he stack it up, build his reserves, and never tell Stacey thing one about his arrangements, his holdings, his obligations?

So here she is with all these questions:

"Why? When? Where? What? And how many more months do I sit in the lawyer's office asking, not understanding, wondering? Sure, I know it will all work out eventually and I also know how lucky I am compared to some women. But do you know what bothers me most? Mostly I guess what bothers me is that I can't help wondering, asking, why would Virgil do me this way?"

Martha: Of course, that would register especially with a woman, and it did with me. After our first listening to Stacey's frustration, I took Charlie to my desk and told him we'd better have a long look together. Our problem is that I keep the books and he doesn't know thing one about our finances. And the truth is he really doesn't care. If he has some pocket change, a few

111

dollars in his billfold, he seems to be thinking. "Don't bother me with all these peccadillos."

So I leveled with him, told him how helpless he would be if something happened to me. I'm in good health, and I'm looking forward to a long time in this marriage. Yet I knew I would feel better if he'd take a serious look at all our money matters. So he did (sort of) and I do feel better (sort of) because knowing about money *is* important for both husband *and* wife. Or in some cases like ours, it is also important for both wife *and* husband.

SEPARATE BANK ACCOUNTS

Herly and Ag have been staying in love for thirty-eight years. They have an unusual procedure for handling their money. She doesn't work, but every month they divide his check down the middle. They have separate bank accounts and each one has certain obligations, certain bills to be paid as their responsibility.

They say it's been great for them because it gives them each some definite assignment, plus independence, plus that all important freedom to

use their own judgment.
Plus fun.

Fun? Yes, fun. They take
turns grocery shopping. He
buys one week at his favorite
store, she buys next week
at hers.

So what comes of that?
"One of the good things
is we have so much fun
bragging, arguing, kidding.
Who got the real bargains?
My grocer is better than
your grocer."

Maybe the slogan should
be: "It really isn't how much
you have. It's how much fun
you have with what you have
that makes the difference!"

RECEIPT FOR ONE CUP OF COFFEE?

Dear Dr. and Mrs. Shedd:

Do you think it's right for a man to have complete
charge of all the money? My husband won't even tell
me how much he makes, and that's not the worst part.
The worst part is that every month I heve to sit down
and explain everything I spend out of my allowance,
and I do mean everything.

And would you believe this? Recently when I
couldn't remember one little item, he told me that from
now on I'd have to get a receipt for everything.

Can you imagine getting a receipt for a thirty-cent
cup of coffee? If I was a spendthrift or a careless buyer,

I might be able to understand, but I'm not. From the time I was a little girl, my parents trained me to manage money.

When I tell my husband he's treating me like a child and I don't like all this reporting, he just shrugs and says that's the way all the men do it in his family. Well, lately I have been thinking this through and I don't like the feelings I get. What I feel is that when a man has so little respect for a woman, a woman loses respect for him. Honestly, I am wondering about our future, because he refuses to compromise or to counsel with anyone or to give any indication that he cares how I feel.

Is there anything I can do?

Very little you can do. If he won't face the fact that he is badly in error, then your options are limited to: (1) learning to live with it; (2) deciding whether you love him enough to make all the adjustments on your side.

By every means possible, keep him facing the fact that his lack of respect for your good judgment is destroying your respect for him—and let's hope the message gets through. No woman treated forever like a chattel is likely to stay forever in love.

THE CHARLIE AND MARTHA METHOD

Early in our marriage we found ourselves fussing too much about money. We fussed at the bills, fussed at the budget, fussed at each other. But even worse, we felt an inner fussing when we weren't fussing externally.

One of us was brought up in a home where the note was worry, worry, worry. The other grew up with strict application of "never buy anything you can't pay cash for." Here we were with debts beaucoup—miscellaneous debts, school debts, charge accounts, and not enough money to cover all those payments.

What could we do?

More money was not our answer right then, because we knew there was no more money in our immediate future. But we better do something quick, something colossal.

That's when we decided to adopt a system and stay with it. For thirty-five years we've lived by our Charlie and Martha method and for us it's the absolute ultimate.

The Method:

Give 10%   Save 10%   Spend the rest
with thanksgiving and praise.

Questionnaire on Money and How We Handle It

Since "talk, talk, talk" is one of the major secrets to staying in love, the questionnaires in this book are designed to facilitate conversation. Unless otherwise indicated, we suggest that you each answer the questions on your own separate papers. Then if your marriage is ready for it, study each other's answers, compare notes, and set a time for discussion.

1. Which has the best background for money management?
   I do_____
   My mate does_____
   We both have good backgrounds_____
   Differences in our backgrounds are _____

2. Who worries most about money?
   I do_____
   My mate_____
   We both worry too much_____

3. When the sounds of complaining are heard (expenditures, bills, debts, and where does it all go) most of the complaints come from:
   Me_____
   My mate_____
   We both complain too much_____

4. Overextension is a habit which can cause big problems (unwise use of credit cards, too many charge accounts, piling up debts). I think this is a problem with us.
   Yes_____
   No_____
   I tend too much in this direction.
   Yes_____
   No_____
   My mate does.
   Yes_____
   No_____

116

5. To better our overall money picture:
   We could cut down the following expenditures:

   _____

   _____

   We could increase our income by:

   _____

   _____

6. The poverty complex can be another problem. Sometimes this results in plain old stinginess. Tight is another word for it. I sometimes tend in this direction.
   Yes_____
   No_____
   My mate does.
   Yes_____
   No_____

7. We designate one item in our budget just for fun.
   Yes_____
   No_____

8. We are adequately insured.
   Yes_____
   No_____

9. We have agreed to a definite system of money management, and we live by it.
   Yes_____
   No_____

10. By the formula: "Save 10%, Give 10%, Spend the rest with thanksgiving and praise," our record is:
    Giving_____%
    Saving_____%
    Spending_____%

15
Fun

"Where Have All the Flowers Gone?"

"WHERE HAVE ALL THE FLOWERS GONE?"

For us "Where Have All the Flowers Gone?" is more than the title of a popular song. It's a question we ask ourselves on occasion and always it leads us to questions like these:

Have we let some of our little fun things get away?

Are we focusing so much on the big, good times we're passing over the small ones?

Should we renew some of the old hobbies we enjoyed, backtrack to some of our former, simple pleasures?

From our mail, seminars, stories couples have told us, and out of our own living room, come the following vignettes:

"We never have fun anymore. It's all business and bills and dumb social engagements.

121

Last week we stopped to see Ross and Jennifer. I guess they're the best friends we ever had, only we almost never have time to see them. Do you know what they were doing when we got there? Playing Scrabble, just the two of them. I've thought about that so much and every time I think about it, I almost want to cry."

Johnny and Edith are in their kitchen tonight. They're making jellies and jams together and this is only one small part of their fun. They have become pickers of berries and cherries and grapes and plums and apples and oranges and grapefruit and nuts. They have also become blenders superb of concoctions delectable. But if you could visit their kitchen right now you would sense another kind of blending. This is togetherness of a special kind. Gathering, creating, giving to friends. And one way to spell it is
FUN!

Ask Thelma and Gordon, "What's fun for you?" and they would answer:
"When we first started out, we were really poor. Or at least we thought we were and every month we just got by. Then one Christmas someone gave us one of these 'paint-by-number pictures.' Well, we had the best time doing that thing together. So we got a bank and saved our pennies and when we had

enough, we'd go shopping, buy another picture. Of course, you know by now we don't have to save our pennies, but we do. Then when we get enough, we go shopping, buy another picture and I suppose we'll be saving our pennies and buying pictures and painting by numbers as long as we live. Why? Because for us it's real fun!"

There is a special fascination in seashells. How did this one come by its lavish colors and that by its strange shape? Mystery! Wonder! What creature of the sea lived here and where is that creature now?

For the thirteen years of their marriage Mark and Anna have been studying seashells, collecting seashells, and spending time together along the shore. This year is a special seashell year for Mark and Anna. This is the year they've been planning so long. Vacation on an exotic island known for its lovely songs, beauty, and romance. And seashells.

"You've heard the old saying, If you can't beat 'em, join 'em. Well, my version is, If you can't beat 'em, ask 'em to join you.

"Now the reason I am writing is something that happened two years ago. I'm into sailing big and when I first got into it, I must say my wife wasn't exactly overjoyed, me being gone, and all.

"Then one day I was out there sailing and I got this great idea. Why not teach her to crew for me?

"Well, she went for that right away and she has gotten so good that last week we won third in the regatta and you should see our trophy. I never won anything like that when just my friends were crewing for me.

"How come it took me so long to ask her?"

We once visited a campground and did our own survey on "Why are you here? What does camping do for you?"

"We can't afford to stay in motels. Camping out is cheaper." (Is it really?)

"You meet the most interesting people when you're camping."

"We like nature." (Ants, mosquitoes, bugs. You like them too?)

"Another thing is you can go places other people never get to go."

"I guess for us it's the togetherness. We each have our chores. Setting up, packing up, pitching in, getting along. (Well most of the time we get along.)"

But here's the reason we liked best:

"I'm eighty-one now and the Missus is seventy-six. We know one of these years we won't be able to camp anymore. I guess at our age one answer to why we do it is thinking back on all the good times."

"BEHOLD HOW GREAT A MATTER"

Why do marriages break up? One answer is "boredom." The zest is gone.

So how do we keep it?

In our marriage the zest is most likely to come on padded feet. No announcement. There it is. Quiet. Nice. And when we ask, "Why do we feel this glow together?" the answers are often so simple. Like hobbies we share.

If you could see our wall of jigsaw puzzles, you would say, "That's exciting. Look at this one. Look at that one. Fascinating." (Did you know they make glue for preserving puzzles so you can hang them on the wall?)

But to us they're much, much more than an unusual wall of unusual pictures. They're shopping together in many places, mementos of trips we've taken, sights we've seen; good times to remember.

Yet more than anything they're quiet evenings of fun. Or fun with the whole family. "Hey! Let's work a puzzle."

Why do some couples stay in love? Could it be we spend too much, go too much, look too far for big, big answers? We've had some colossal times, real majors to remember, and you have. But when we ask, "How can we keep the glow?" isn't one small answer the small fun times?

Straight from The Book: "Behold how great a matter a little fire kindleth." James 3:5 (KJ)

"I WISH WE WERE POOR AGAIN"

Sally and Elmer started on a shoestring and made it

big. They were a determined couple, they worked hard, and they went straight to the top. Elmer ran a smooth operation, Sally kept the books and everything they did seemed to come out money.

Then one day Sally came to see us. Over the coffee cups she shared her deepest feelings.

"I wish we were poor again and isn't that an awful thing to say. But honestly we hardly ever see each other alone anymore and all we talk about is business. Anytime we're out together, we're checking new products, checking our salesmen, entertaining customers."

Then she began to muse on the years of their early marriage. Their attic apartment; evenings together on their second-hand sofa, listening to their tiny radio; talking; loving.

"Sometimes we would go for a walk, window shopping. We might even treat ourselves to a cheap movie."

Then said the lady with everything, "Seems we have all we ever dreamed except the one thing I always wanted—to be together."

More questions for staying in love:

> Are we pressing too hard for the future and missing the good things today?
>
> Have we placed so much value on lesser things that we're losing our togetherness?

"UNPACK THE SUITCASE"

Luther is on his way up. He's done well with his company, and one of the requirements for advancement has been a series of moves.

So? Countless people move these days, and often. But here are a few lines from Luther with some special thoughts on moving.

"This last time we moved, we decided something I'd like to share. We had moved so often we'd fallen into the bad habit of what we call 'temporary living,' and it actually sneaked up on us almost before we knew it. The way we finally recognized it is that we caught ourselves asking, 'Why get involved in the church or the school or the community? Why make friends or knock ourselves out to get acquainted? Why bother with neighbors? We won't be here long. We'll be moving again soon.'

"Then my wife came on an old clipping she'd saved, and it had one line in it which got us thinking. Fact is, this simple phrase changed our attitude completely. And the phrase is 'unpack the suitcase and live.'

"We don't know who wrote it, but he said that he and his family had moved a lot too and now suddenly they realized they'd missed too much.

"So his advice was, 'The day you arrive on a new scene, start living. Go meet your neighbors, find a church, make some friends, get with it right where you are right now.'

"Anyway, my wife and I thought this through and we decided he was talking to us. This 'temporary living' we'd been into was strictly no good. No good for the kids. No good for our marriage. From now on we would do what the man said, 'Unpack the suitcase and live.'"

16
Sex

Celebration in the Bedroom

LISTENING TOO MUCH TO THE EXPERTS?

"My wife and I decided some time ago we were getting buried under too much advice and especially about sex. We had been working so hard trying to do all the things we heard about that we didn't have time for the things we liked.

"We had been reading books, attending lectures, going to workshops and trying like crazy to do the things *they* said. But all of a sudden we realized we were happier when we were doing things our way. So we decided to heck with it, we'd go back to being ourselves.

"When you asked for people to write about staying in love, we thought we better put in our two-cents worth. Of course, there may be couples who need help more than we did, but if you're like us, sometimes it's better to tune out all the advice and just let it happen."

131

THE MISSIONARY

"I love my husband but sometimes I get so turned off and one of those times is when he keeps pressuring me to feel the way he feels about sex. Do you know the term 'one-hundred megaton climax'? We read it somewhere and we like it. But what gets me is that he acts so wounded if I don't respond one-hundred megaton every time. Well, sometimes I don't want to, because I don't need to. Why does he keep pressuring me so hard to do it his way?"

What's the answer? One answer for us was that day when Martha made another of her memorable speeches:

"Now hear this, Charlie. Your understanding of sex is too one-sided. Apparently no one has ever educated you in the very solid truth that women are not men.

"I will now explain how it is with me. I do not need a cataclysmic reaction every time. If you will let me, sometimes I will merely enjoy you enjoying me. Part of the time even the warmest woman likes nothing more than to feel like a missionary. Could you possibly calm your pressure tactics enough to think this through and see what happens?"

What happened was extra-extra. New meanings, new pleasures, and sex at its best for both of us, celebration par excellence.

And a further thought from Martha (especially for young wives):

"I am well aware that certain so-called experts say both male and female should respond one-hundred percent one-hundred percent of the time.

"So what's wrong with that?

"What's wrong is that these so-called experts are not right.

"If a woman's sexual feelings are enough for her, and her husband likes her as she is, what could be better than that?"

ARE ALL SEX FANTASIES EVIL?

"Are all sex fantasies evil?"

The question comes from a Florida housewife, a mother, "lucky to be married to a great guy" (her words), and she must be a beautiful person. Honesty like hers is beautiful anywhere.

Yet at one point she's struggling.

"My husband and I are happily married and we have a good relationship in every way, including sex. But sometimes I have fantasies about other men. Do you understand what I mean? They are only flashes, but believe me very real.

"Because we have always been open with each other, I have told my husband that I have these thoughts. But he says not to worry, because fantasies are natural, and they might even be a good thing. Do you think this could be true?"

Yes, this could be true. Sex fantasies can be negative when they become a driving force to negative involvements outside marriage. But our experience is that they can also be a plus when controlled, d scussed, understood, and then put where they belong.

How much should we surface? Should we go into detail? Doesn't it depend on how much guilt we feel, the tension inside, and what our marriage can stand?

Here, from another letter, is the perfect answer:

"The nicest thing happened recently. I had some things on my mind which had really been bothering me. So finally I said, 'Mark, I need someone to talk to about certain feelings I have and I'm talking about guilt feelings. Do you think you can stand it now if I tell you what's bothering me? Would you love me just as much?'

"Do you know what he said? He said, 'Funny you'd bring that up right now. Real funny, because I've been thinking maybe I needed help from you. And I've been wondering if I told you, would you love me just as much?'"

Play the record one more time: nobody can say for sure what's right for everyone. How could "they" possibly know exactly what we need? Yet for the greatest of loves this is a fact:

The more we know each other, the more we love!

GRACE

Because the fear of self-revelation is a very human tendency, there is one basic requirement for opening up to each other. "Grace" is a theological word which stands for "the free unmerited love and favor of God."

Jesus said many things about our Heavenly Father, but are any words more amazing than these? "No matter where we have been, what we have done, or how far the country we have wandered—*God loves us anyway.*"

This is grace, and in the finest of marriages there is this deep understanding: "If you have memories which make you nervous, recollections about some awful part of you, you don't need to be afraid. You can tell me these if you like and I'll only love you more, because I'll know you better."

Grace enables us to share another thing:

"Could it possibly be that some of our far-out ideas might be worked into things worthwhile?

"I have this dream about me, see! In this dream I'm somebody special and doing things I can hardly believe. Great accomplishments. Let me tell you about my high hopes, goals I have never reached. And would you also like to know of the times when I was really proud of myself, bigger than anyone knows? Plus some of my thoughts are so beautiful they seem almost too far-out to muse on, but would you muse with me?"

So sharing our negatives is only a part of total knowing. The more we share those negatives, the more we uncover the "fine" in us. "This too we are. Let us now be grander together than we had ever dreamed."

What does all this have to do with sex? For us the answer is: Everything! Wise couples know that foreplay is much more than physical stimulation. Foreplay is also visit, visit, visit. At the kitchen table, in the living room, riding together in the car, wherever circuits are being cleared by conversation, these same circuits are also being cleared for a more exciting sex life.*

Adapted from the book, Celebration in the Bedroom, *by Charlie and Martha Shedd, Word, Inc. 1979, pages 50–51.*

Questionnaire on Celebration in the Bedroom

Since "talk, talk, talk" is one of the major secrets to staying in love, the questionnaires in this book are designed to facilitate conversation. Unless otherwise indicated, we suggest that you each answer the questions on your own separate papers. Then if your marriage is ready for it, study each other's answers, compare notes, and set a time for discussion.

1. On a scale of zero to ten rate the following (ten for perfect):
    Our overall sex life_____
    My attitude_____
    My mate's_____
2. Our frequency pattern is:
    Okay_____
    Not often enough_____
    Too often_____
3. Some of my hang-ups are _____
    I think my mate has hang-ups about _____
4. We have thoroughly discussed our sexual backgrounds; our early training; things which happened to us; mistaken ideas.
    Yes_____
    No_____
5. I believe I am fully aware of both physical and emotional differences between male and female.
    Yes_____
    No_____
6. By discussion, by body language, by signals, we let our wants be known and meet each other's needs.
    Yes_____
    No_____
    Improving_____
7. Something new I would like to try is_____
    _____

17
The Years Ahead

"Staying in Love
Is Never Finished"

THE MOBILE HOME "PARK"(?)

"Do you know what a Mobile Home Park is? Well, I've got news for you. It isn't trees and a stream and green grass and picnic places. What it really means is that we're 'parked' here permanently overlooking a lot of other mobile homes 'parked' here. And if you want to know what togetherness means, this is it.

"So why are we here? Because it's all we can afford in our retirement, that's why, and, yes, we do feel closed in compared to the big house we moved from and, yes, we do get on each other's nerves.

"But it isn't as bad as it was at first and I'll tell you why it isn't so bad. One day we had a long talk, took a look at exactly how we felt, and then we agreed that after forty years this retirement time was no time for not getting along. We decided we would go back to some of the little courtesies we started with, some of the good-time things we did when we were first married. And it's gone a lot better.

139

"When we read your request for people's ideas on how to stay in love, we thought we should write and say staying in love, at least for us, isn't finished just because we've finished working, and what is more, we know it probably never will be."

Item worth a retake: "We went back to some of the little courtesies we started with, some of the good-time things we did when we were first married."

Uncanny how often one letter arrives and almost in the same mail a second comes sounding similar notes. Close on the heels of that "Mobile Home" letter came this from a wise husband:

"You know what has helped me to stay in love as I've grown older? It's remembering why I fell in love in the first place; seeing my wife the way she was when I first knew her; recapturing some of that feeling. You think this would make me lonesome for the good old days? It really doesn't. Instead it actually makes me realize how much more beautiful she is today; how much more we have going for us now."

RULES FOR A FUN RETIREMENT

What are the secrets to successful retirement?

The Johnsons live in Tennessee, both sixty-six, and this is the word from their house:

"We have friends for whom retirement is really awful, but we decided ahead of time to work out some rules we would try to live by. Thought you might like them.

"1. We'll decide right now that 'togetherness' will be easier with some mini-vacations from each other. Example? Husband runs the errands—post office, bank, cleaner, grocery. (Men can learn to shop even if they've never done it.) Wife does her telephoning while he's gone. We would also develop some individual friendships and each do some things we like to do without the other.

"2. We would have a good session now and then on what attracted us to each other in the first place. What did we enjoy doing when we were courting and in the years gone by? Attending plays, square dancing, bridge, bowling, tennis, swimming, concerts, anything that was fun back there; we should try these again, because maybe we might still enjoy them.

"3. We agreed to make up for lost time such as talking like we'd never talked before; learning new things about each other; going places we'd only thought about; reading books we'd been wanting to read and then discussing what we read.

"4. We would become part of retirement groups such as American Association for Retired People, etc. But we would not limit our friendships to folks our own age. We have found that children, teenagers, and even young couples do enjoy people our age, and we sure enjoy them for a fresh breeze.

"5. Finally (and most important) we decided to rediscover religion. One of the happiest surprises for us has been learning how up-to-date the church has gotten since we were active years ago. As we got interested in the church, we decided to adopt our own small mission project. For instance, once each week we make calls together in our church's home for the elderly. Amazing how this makes us appreciate our good health and we always feel better for having made someone else feel better.

141

"But probably our most exciting project lately was when our pastor asked us to give a talk for our senior citizens' group. That is when we wrote down our rules and we have given them in several other places. They have been so well received and we have become so excited about them that this may be why we thought you might like them too."

WHEN THE LAST CHILD LEAVES HOME

Dear Dr. Shedd:

My wife gets so depressed sometimes. I'm really worried. Alice Ann is getting married this June, and she's the last of our four children to leave home. Now this is no melancholy woman I'm married to, but sometimes I catch her with that far-off look and I know what she's thinking. This happened to one of our friends a year ago, and for them it's been a disaster.

You must hear from people who are going through this and what do they do?

The Johnsons started furniture refinishing last year. They've always enjoyed hunting antiques, visiting out-of-the-way places, turning up old pieces, and now they're beginning to think that someday they'll make it a business. He repairs, fits, glues, rebuilds. She does the sanding, staining, varnishing. Their youngest child is a high-school senior and they've always been a strong family. Of course, no antique, no old piece of furniture could mean what the children mean. But it

142

could "take up some slack" as the Johnsons put it.

We recently heard a psychiatrist say, "If parents develop their maximum oneness during the earlier years, when their last child leaves home, a new emotion sets in. It is called 'ecstasy.'"

Staying in love in the "passages" may often depend on looking ahead, planning ahead for a new kind of togetherness.

Roger and Sue:

"We don't have any big secrets to staying in love. Mostly for us it's little things over the years.

"For instance, one of our rituals when the children were small (and even after they were teens) was a lot of good, solid visiting every night around our dinner table. We'd talk and plan and laugh and hear each other's problems. Of course, it wasn't every night, but we all counted this time so important we would plan our schedules for it.

"You asked about 'togetherness' secrets after the kids are grown. Well, we have one.

"Every night, every single night except in rare emergencies, we have dinner together at the big table. No TV, no quick meals at the kitchen counter, no exceptions (except maybe a backyard picnic or dinner out now and then at one of our favorite restaurants).

"You see what this means? What it means

is that we determined we wouldn't let the best things about our relationship get away from us even if we were alone. We would carry on just like always. So that's why I say, for us staying in love is staying with the things that meant so much in the first place."

Questionnaire on the Years Ahead

Since "talk, talk, talk" is one of the major secrets to staying in love, the questionnaires in this book are designed to facilitate conversation. Unless otherwise indicated, we suggest that you each answer the questions on your own separate papers. Then if your marriage is ready for it, study each other's answers, compare notes, and set a time for discussion.

1. Our tendency as a couple is:
   Live today and let the future take care of itself
   _____
   We worry so much about the future that we miss too much living right now_____

2. I look forward to the retirement years when we will have more time. Our hobbies (shared hobbies) which can carry over into the future are _____
   _____, _____

3. We talk about our future, enjoy dreaming, planning together:
   Yes_____
   No_____
   If not, why don't we? _____
   Some of the things we might do together when we are free from family responsibility are _____
   _____

4. "I'm So Much More Beautiful Every Day I Can Hardly Wait Till Friday." Silly. Maybe not. Am I getting more beautiful?
   Yes_____
   No_____
   Is our relationship becoming more meaningful all the time?
   Yes_____
   No_____

5. My mate is more attractive to me now than during those first years of our marriage.

Yes_____

No_____

How long has it been since I told my mate, "You just go on getting better and better"? _____

18
Religion

Tuning in *Up*

BALANCED THREE WAYS

When we solicited input on "how to stay in love," answers poured in on little things, big things, small secrets, large, plus some from the philosophical.

Here from California is a report called "Balanced Three Ways."

"We have been married twenty years and we are still very much in love. This doesn't make us authorities on the subject, but for us the secret to staying in love and getting the most out of it is keeping our marriage balanced three ways. And the three ways we must keep balanced are:

1. mentally
2. physically
3. spiritually

We notice in your column how often you use the phrase 'talk, talk, talk.' That's how we stay mentally balanced and for us there is no other way.

"So many of our friends seem to relate only on the surface. That's not for us. When our love begins to slip, then we know we haven't been talking enough. So we start in again until we're back on track.

"This means all kinds of talk, small talk and heavy talk. Naturally we have some meaningful times too when we communicate in silence, but those times are more likely to come when we have been talking a lot.

"What do we mean by keeping the physical in balance? We mean staying in shape by exercise, by good eating, by healthy living, and we also make sure we are sexually active enough to meet each other's needs. We think sex is not only beautiful the way it makes us feel toward each other, but it also helps us rest deep and we stay more relaxed in everything we do.

"The third phase of our balance system is spiritual. We belong to a church which we like and attend with some regularity. But for us spiritual balance can also come when we take time to appreciate nature and think about it. Spiritual balance comes too from doing things for other people. Also we may read something good together (or one of us reads to the other) to keep us thinking about the deeper things. We know some couples who have a physical and mental relationship but they lack something. We do too unless we stay in balance spiritually.

"So many marriages breaking up are out of balance but maybe even worse is the fact that many couples are only partially living up to their potential.

"We would feel so good if our thoughts turned out to be a help for someone who needs them. That's why we say for us staying balanced three ways is the answer to staying in love and getting the most out of it."

150

STAYING IN LOVE IS TUNING IN *UP*

"Do you know any way to keep us talking? We agree that communication is important, but our problem is that we don't communicate consistently. It isn't that we can't talk, but we get so busy with the children or our social obligations or working at the church, or we are too tired or something. That's why we are wondering if you know a way to *keep* the lines open."

Yes, we know a way, a way tried and proven; tried and proven for thirty years by the two people we know best. We call it "The Way of the Three Small Signs" and the three small signs are:

A candle

An arrow

Question mark

For thirty years we have been studying the Bible together with our way of the three small signs.

Every day we read from the same passage, same verses, same Book of the Old or New Testaments. We do not read at the same time, because one of us is an early riser. That's Charlie. He's up every day to meet the sun. Even on his day off, he's up bright and early for a full day off. Martha, on the other hand, hardly believes in God before eight-thirty in the morning, plus two cups of coffee. This is why we have our quiet times individually. Same reading, same three signs: candle, arrow, question mark.

The candle means "new light." "This is a first-time thought. Something we've never seen before. Let's discuss."

Question mark: "I don't understand. Help me."

Arrow: "There could be a flaw in me here; a negative

in my background; I am not what I should be." (WARN-ING: We only use arrow signs for ourselves. Sure, we may be thinking "I hope she gets this" or "He needs that." But with us, sins big and little are first a very personal matter. So the right of self-discovery is all-important.)

Now having marked, we sit together for a session and compare notes. We talk, talk, talk, discuss, speculate, research, laugh, argue, and we never come out of a session like this without knowing each other better, respecting each other more, loving each other with a new love.

Twenty times in thirty years we've been through the Bible using this method. For us this is the ultra of communication, the activator of love at its very best.

So here is the question of questions for Charlie and Martha and everyone asking, "How can we stay in love?"

If God is love
as the Good Book says,
wouldn't our love
be more Divine
if we spent more time
with the Source?